Reach Out
and TOUCH

Dr. Warren Jean Rouse

WestBow
PRESS®
A DIVISION OF THOMAS NELSON
& ZONDERVAN

WestBow Press books may be ordered through booksellers or by contacting:

WestBow Press
A Division of Thomas Nelson & Zondervan
1663 Liberty Drive
Bloomington, IN 47403
www.westbowpress.com
1 (866) 928-1240

Interior Image Credit: Tony Anderson

ISBN: 978-1-9736-6612-7 (sc)
ISBN: 978-1-9736-6613-4 (e)

Library of Congress Control Number: 2019943810

Print information available on the last page.

WestBow Press rev. date: 8/5/2019

Dedication

Ask the Lord to bless your plans, and you will be successful in carrying them out.
Proverbs 16:3 GNT

My Encouragers

My Lord and Savior Jesus Christ – Salvation &Inspiration
My Husband – Motivation
Biological Family – Exhortation
Church Family – Cultivation and Consolation
Career Family - Stimulation
Friends – Invigoration

Thanks for being a part of my Life's Journey
Numbers 6:24 – 26 NIV
"May the Lord bless you and keep you;
May the Lord make his face shine on you and be gracious to you;
May the Lord turn his face toward you and give you peace."

Contents

Section I - Biblical Encouragers

Section II - Emotional Encouragers

Section III - Motivational Encouragers

Section IV - Christian Education

Section V - Praise and Worship

Section VI - Events and Tributes

Section VII - A Star is Born

Acknowledgments

Special Thanks to the Lord God Almighty for endowing me with the gift to express myself through the written word.

A loving expression of gratitude I give to, James Rouse, the love of my life for fifty-five years and an encouraging friend, Thelma Shorter. They both started encouraging me years ago to write a book because they had observed writings that I had done for the school, church, events and special occasions. I only saw my writings as something that I loved doing not as an opportunity to write a book.

I owe a debt of appreciation to two teachers who planted the seed of confidence in the heart of a very shy and timid child. During the early years of my young life, my sixth-grade elementary music teacher, Mrs. Calloway, used my poem as our sixth-grade graduation song using the tune of "Love is a Many Splendored Thing." The title of my poem was "School is a Many Splendored Thing." My high school English teacher, Mrs. Opal Harper, would always tell me that I was a profound thinker because it was reflected and expressed in my writing. She just passed away a few years ago, and I regret that I didn't show my appreciation. They will never know how those small gestures influenced my literary life.

I'm grateful for two other young ladies on my literary journey, Bettie Thomas and Kaye Rainey. They kept me abreast of resources that would come across their desk with information about poetry and literary workshops or events. The information that I received helped me to share my thoughts, ideas, and poetry with others who were aspiring authors and those who had already written their first book.

I recognize my family; my children, and grandchildren and their spouses, great-grandchildren, my siblings, and their spouses for their support. They always encouraged me in whatever task I set my mind to do. Mrs. Pinky, my granddaughter, is also a poet and hopefully, she will continue the writing tradition along with other descendants who may be blessed with the gift to write. Encouragement is such a useful and inexpensive tool of the tongue for helping, building, repairing, creating and designing the lives of others aware and unaware. The seed of encouragement continues for many years even after we have departed.

I salute my church, Mt. Calvary Missionary Baptist Church family for allowing me the opportunities throughout the years to write plays and to use my poetry for resolutions and acknowledgments during funeral services, and special church events and programs. Those opportunities helped me to mature in my writing and kept my creativity fresh. I have included a particular poem that I wrote several years ago when we celebrated our church anniversary program.

A SALUTE TO MT. CALVARY MISSIONARY BAPTIST CHURCH

A Salute to My Church of 55 Years

MT. CALVARY CHURCH WE CARE AND WE SHARE
Like a beacon of light people often stop by.
Sometime we think and wonder why.
Other churches they seem to zip pass,
But we're among their top choices and not their last.
They come from far, near and everywhere,
Because Mt. Calvary Church we care and we share.

For those who are down and out with no place to go,
We carry food, serve, and our Jesus we show.
They may be fearful, stressful, in a shelter for homeless.
But we represent a God who blesses the distress.
For he always hear a cry and prayer.
At Mt. Calvary Church we care and we share.

Jesus never leaves nor does he forsake.
Our voices, our song, our love gifts we take,
To the helpless, and hurting in the nursing home,
Who feels sometimes like all hope has gone,
A sparkle in their eye comes as their burdens we bear.
Mt. Calvary Church we care and we share.

For those who are incarcerated with no place to go.
The deliverer, Jesus, to them we show.
A God of forgiveness is peace and love.
We tell about the strength from high above.
A God who can help make their choices good and fair.
Mt. Calvary Church we care and we share.

We started out with just a kitchen cupboard.
But the needs increased more and more.
With a food pantry we were blessed with much to choose.
For the hungry, down and out, the misused and abused.
We will always be a sun light when clouds hang here and there.
Mt Calvary Church we care and we share.

Our history has produced some of the very best.
Some far and near from the north, south, east and west.
But Mt. Calvary was where the seed was sown.
In the community and world their lights have shown.
It started with the prayers glow and a shining glare.
Mt. Calvary Church we care and we share.

We hope that this part of history will never end.
For this is and has always been the Jesus trend.
Working in love can't be stopped and you can't go wrong.
Jesus caring love is strong, strong, strong.
The world can see Calvary's light from everywhere.
Mt. Calvary Church we care and share

Author – Warren Jean Rouse

Introduction

I started this journey of poetry without the intent of writing a poetry book. I had learned from my teacher in high school that I had a talent for writing. I was in my fifties when the idea began to take root in my internal desire. I went to a poetry writing workshop and was told that my poetry painted a picture. They said the rhyme pattern was not current for this time and he gave me a new model to use. I became a little disenchanted because this was the personal style that I had adapted to for the last fifty years, Old School. Since other people were being encouraged by the poetry that I had sent to them, this encouragement ignited my desire to continue my writings in my own personal style.

I always had an empathetic, sensitivity toward those with heartache, distress, and pain. One year it seemed to have been several deaths, and I knew holidays were hard times for those who had experienced a loss. I wrote and sent a poem to as many as I could remember for that year. This desire gave birth to my first grief poem, "Memories of Christmas Past" and this poem started my holiday ministry outreach.

I started my personal prison ministry communicating with young men in our community who had been incarcerated and had been mentored by my husband. Guided by the Holy Spirit and my personal relationship with Jesus Christ, I felt that they needed to know someone cared in spite of the mistakes they had made. It was also a way to show them that Jesus still loved and cared about them by letting his light shine through me when I shared my poems. I also used my poetry as I ministered in the nursing homes and other places where there were hurting, sick, hopeless, and helpless who were facing sorrow, pain, and other tragedies.

My poetry writing expanded to other special occasions and events. Whenever we had our monthly family reunion meetings, we celebrated the monthly birthdays. I'm a busy bee, and I would always forget to buy a card so I would quickly write a birthday poem. I also wrote poems for church activities, services, funeral resolutions, acknowledgments, presentations, and other special events. Special events are avenues to express the social part of man and serves as an outlet for emotional, physical, and spiritual healing. Throughout the years, I accumulated and sent out many poems I never kept copies because computers and copy machines were not as accessible as they are now. I'm thankful to have an opportunity to share them with others through my book.

I planned to write a book when I retired. I pondered for some time trying to decide whether to write the poetry book or another book that I had in mind. I had written several titles and even chapters for several other publications that had come to my mind. I finally decided to write a book of poetry. My empathy had become more in-depth as I worked teaching and counseling children for thirty-eight years. I taught twelve years and spent the rest of my career counseling elementary students with their own set of pain, problems, lack of confidence and self-image. With God and the Holy Spirit as my guide, I will continue to reach out to hurting people and encourage others to do so as well while reading the poetic expressions in this book.

After I retired, I went back to school to further my Christian education at GMOR Seminary Institute. I received my doctorate in Christian Counseling just as I had received my masters in counseling in the secular culture. I am presently working on my Ph.D. in Christian Education an unfinished degree before my doctorate in Christian Education. I sometimes perceive my poetry as a continued opportunity to counsel in the written form. This is indeed my desire. To God Be the Glory!

ESSENTIAL CLEANING AIDES FOR THE SPIRIT, SOUL & MIND

Sponge/Spirit

Squeeze out the gossip, greed, guilt as you wipe up the grease and grime.
Soak in the gospel, gratefulness and giving.

Gloves/Soul

Protect by washing out bacteria of bitterness, baggage & burdens.
Rinse out germs with forgiveness, confession, & praise.

Hyssop Tea/Body

Clean out laziness, excessive eating & being a busy bee.
Work out with exercise, proper diet, sleep & rest.

TRASH BAG / SPIRIT, SOUL & BODY

Trash excess television, telephone, texting & talking.
Treat eye and ear gate with the word, worship, & witnessing.

SPIRIT MIND AND BODY SPRING CLEANING

1. Glass cleaner –Use this glass cleaner to clean the eyes of the body. Clean and get the mote out of your own eyes so that you can see clearly on how to get the mote out of someone else's eyes. Sis. Bernita Dedmond
2. Dust Spray – This dust spray is good for the mind cleaning. Spray, meditate and think on things of the gospel instead of things of the gossip. Clean out the cob wells of the mind. Sis. Mary Bennett
3. Furniture Polish – Polish and shine, shine, shine. Brighten up your spirit man by Praying daily and glow with the glory and light of Jesus. Sis. Carolyn Adams
4. Clorox – Holy, Holy, Holy Lord God Almighty. Be washed white by confessing and repenting. He shall wash away your sins and you shall be as white as snow.
5. Carpet Cleaner – Read the word daily. Walk and witness with the word of God. Use your body in the work of service, and you shall tread upon the Lion and adder and trample them under your feet.

BIBLICAL ENCOURAGERS

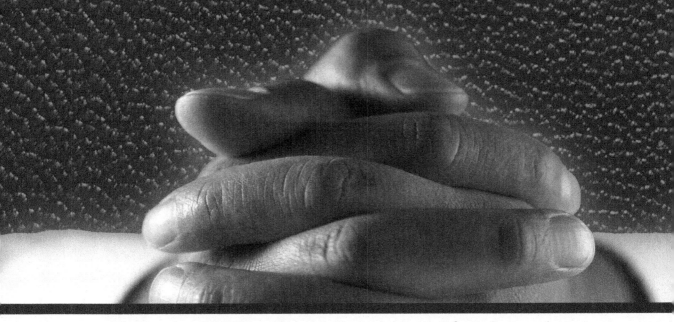

Your word is a lamp unto my feet and a light unto my path. Psalms 119:105 KJV

Biblical Encouragers Word Message

BELIEFS

INSPIRATIONALLY

BENEFITTING

LIBERALLY

IMPROVING

CHRISTIANS

AMAZING

LIFESTYLES

EXHORTING

NEWBORN

CHRISTIANS

OFFERING

UNFAILING

RIGHTEOUSNESS

ATONEMENT

GUARANTEEING

EVERLASTING

REDEMPTIVE

SALVATION

Beattitudes of Blessings Word Message

BLESS THOSE WHO SEEK
ELEVATE THE MEEK
APPRECIATE THE PURE IN HEART
TREASURE THE POOR IN SPIRIT
THANK THE PEACEMAKERS
ILLUMINATE THE MERCIFUL
TOUCH THE MOURNFUL
UNDERSTAND THE PERSECUTED
DESIRES WATER FOR THE THIRSTY
ENCOURAGE THE HUNGRY
SUPPORT THE POOR

My Poor Spirit Must Seek the Rich King of the Kingdom

When you feel inside like something is missing.
You want to see, but then you start resisting.
Thinking it's something you really need to eat.
But nothing helps, not even your favorite treat,
It's like a hollow sound from the beat of a drum,
My poor spirit must seek the rich king of the kingdom.

Oh, the spirit and the flesh, the spirit, and the flesh.
The two oh no cannot come together and mesh.
I fill my belly, but my spirit needs more.
How can I feel the center of my spiritual core?
I must search from where the answer may come.
My poor spirit must seek the rich king of the kingdom.

Even the earth's riches of silver and gold,
Doesn't bring the warmth for I still feel the cold.
I know that God's wealth can only comfort and satisfy.
His treasured word helps me to soar and like an eagle fly high.
I know now where the true and divine riches come from.
My weak spirit must seek the rich king of the kingdom.

I must continue to fill my spirit each and every day.
As I meditate in the word daily in a consecrated way.
Seeking and knowing the spiritual wealth that I have found,
Is in the here and now and also where I'm bound.
My fullness of peace, love, and joy is satisfying and awesome.
My poor spirit sought and found the rich king of the kingdom.

Comfort Will Come to Those Who Mourn

When the heart is broken, it's a funny thing.
Our voice can't even find a song to sing.
Feeling only pieces of death, sorrow, emptiness, and grief,
Nothing found seems to bring a healing relief.
Fragments are pulled apart as if tattered and torn.
But comfort will come to those who mourn.

I'm seeking hard and looking for just a little light.
To turn my darkness into something vibrant and bright,
My illuminated mind remembers I will never leave or forsake you.
God's revived refreshing is like the morning dew.
I will cast my care on him as a babythat's newborn.
Remembering comfort will come to those who mourn.

If I wait on the Lord my strength, he will renew,
Every step of the way will propel me through.
A sweeping of my joy will come in the morning.
Like a new garment gorgeous, beautiful and adorning.
Appearing as a rainbow after a thunderous storm
Comfort will come to those who mourn.

I will now exalt his name with a prayer and praise!
The cheer in my heart has now been raised.
The broken parts of my heart are now back together.
In spite of all the tears of rain during my stormy weather,
With moments of peace and glory, I can loudly blow my horn!
My comfort has now come as one who has mourned.

The Earth Will Belong to All Who Are Meek

There is much in our power to think, say, or do.
We recognize that it can be channeled through me and you.
The meek knows who truly has control.
Submitting to the God who sits on the throne of gold,
It's called power under control and not a sign of one who's weak.
Because the earth will belong to all, who are meek.

There is no reason when you're right to have to defend.
From the unfair criticism, let no revenge be your trend.
Just wait on God he's got your back.
With his power, you cease fire without an attack.
Pray fervently for the humility they should seek.
Because the earth will belong to all, who are meek.

Free from the frenzy you calmly wait.
Forsaking wrath, condemnation, malice, and hate.
With a soft, gentle answer, you're quiet, and you're still.
Attacks many times come to those who are in God's will.
Just look up high to the mountainside peak.
Because the earth will belong to all, who are meek.

Recognize that God controls all of our affairs.
When feeling overwhelmed cast on him all of your cares.
God will exalt you, and in their presence, you will be strong.
He will shine the light on your righteousness and highlight their wrong.
Trust in him when things seem to be hopeless and bleak.
Because the earth will belong to all, who are meek.

A Righteous Thirst and Hunger Can Bring Satisfaction

We search, and we seek a good life in all the wrong places.
Like running a marathon in so many races,
Winning a lot seems like I'm always failing.
With an empty and dry shouting whining and wailing,
I realize now that all of this was only a distraction.
I needed a righteous thirst and hunger to bring satisfaction.

Clothes, cars, and money left me empty, and happiness was rare.
I kept looking for what I needed by searching here and there.
I looked and saw a lady in the last place with a big smile.
I was confused by her smile as she ran each and every mile,
At the finishing line she bows, says, thank you with a loving reaction.
Only a righteous thirst and hunger can bring that kind of satisfaction.

She had sought God in prayer just to get in the race.
For she had been crippled but step by step she kept the pace,
She had pursued the words of God's promise given.
The passion of the Holy Spirit empowered her to be driven.
The pressing and pushing could only come from a spiritual connection.
For only a righteous thirst hunger can bring satisfaction.

Her inner fountain brought a continuous thirst quencher.
Jesus, the Word, our bread of life was her hunger clincher.
Forever learning, knowing, and doing God's will,
Seeking and searching God's way breezed in her calmness still.
Knowing your pace and race is moving you in the right direction.
Only comes with a righteous thirst and hunger that bring satisfaction.

Be Happy to Give and Receive Divine Mercy

Sometimes we wonder why we don't get what we deserve.
It's like someone decided to throw a fastball-curve.
Now we wonder intensely oh what we should do.
Inside our spirit realizing it's free and we can renew.
We seek and look up silently and inwardly to make a decree.
Be happy to give and receive divine mercy.

How can I not give to others what has been given to me?
And not sit in judgment of the mistakes that I see.
My behavior does not always match my desired need.
Therefore I to must let my heart and soul take the lead,
For myself and others, I must quickly fall on my knee.
Be happy to give and receive divine mercy.

My day will come when I won't choose right over wrong.
The mercy train will take me and others on this journey lifelong.
Mercy and grace is God's unmerited gift to defeat sin.
This insight helps all of us to overcome with a victorious win!
Knowledge of this kind does not come from a college degree.
Be happy to give and receive divine mercy.

God's mercy is fresh for us as each morning brings a new day.
It takes a heart of compassion and love when it seems dark and gray.
Mercy we receive with love, and to others we give.
So we will have a peaceful life and thankfully live.
And one day we can share joy happiness and glee.
Be happy to give and receive divine mercy.

The Pure in Heart Shall See God

There is a need for cleansing and purging.
Your heart thumps, thumps, thumps with a strong urging.
God's temple needs to be thoroughly cleaned
From the inside out to be correctly seen,
The journey of a thousand miles takes one step to start.
Let's seek to see God with a pure in heart.

You must first find and see your imperfections.
Looking for God's way to make corrections.
Let Jesus be the mirror that you look through.
To put on the nature of a new you,
Your goal is to become the whole beginning with one part.
Let's seek to see God with a pure in heart.

Talk to God who has the power, kneel sincerely and begin to pray.
Prayer is the key to the path that will lead you the right way.
Cleaning starts from the inside out,
With God's purification, you can now begin to shout,
Let God take his paintbrush and do his work of art.
Let's seek to see God with a pure in heart.

Pray, fast, and read the good book.
Renewing your mind daily for your makeover look,
You can now see what needs a seasonal pruning.
With God's illumination light for excellent grooming.
The spirit in you with holiness now to impart.
Let's seek to see God with a pure in heart.

Make A Place of Contentment and Stillness and Peace

Conflict with self and others can come with any relationship.
We must know how to be quiet and zip our tongue and our lip.
Just being a peaceful person is not ever nearly enough.
We have to know how to help others when things get rough and tough.
Helping life's frustrations, and high flying emotions to decrease,
Let's make a place of contentment and stillness and peace.

Being a problem solver is always the best way to go.
Stop tempers from flaring, and quiet the intense storms that blow.
Learn how to say peace be still to an aggressive situation.
And calmly use God-given skills as solutions to mediation.
We can cause turmoil, strife, and winds of conflict to cease.
Let's make a place of contentment and stillness and peace.

Sometimes things can quickly get wild.
Consult your father's way because you're still his child.
Bring others together and begin a time to pray.
Serenity will begin to come in its own calm and unique way.
Like a caged dove finding his freedom of release.
Let's make a place of contentment and stillness and peace.

Share the peace within that you've found for yourself.
Be sure to include others making sure they are not left.
In Jesus, you've found the peace that everyone needs.
Thank God you know how to plant peaceful mind seeds.
Thoughts from God's word will help tranquility to increase.
Let's make a place of contentment and stillness and peace.

A Heavenly Home for the Righteous Persecuted Nation

There's a place, a place where the weary will cease from troubling!
No more storms and rains causing loud thunderous rumbling!
No more negative, insensitive, criticism and destructive words spoken!
No more reasons to bring tearful, painful hearts to be broken,
For the sake of good, there's no need for heartless critical correction.
There's a heavenly home for the righteous persecuted nation.

There's a place, there is a place where suffering and sorrow will past.
The heavenly kingdom will only forever and eternally last.
No more physical and mental disease, sickness and agonizing pain!
No more death, crying, loss, and grief where only memories remain!
No more war with separation of distant friends and family relation!
There is a heavenly home for the righteous and persecuted nation.

Oh, there's a place, there is a place a home of calm and serene peace.
Where the glory and joy, with a glowing, shining light does not cease!
We will be in awe of the water flowing and glistening crystal clear,
There is nothing and no one to bring the terror of a shaking fear,
The designs of streets with gold and pearly gates attracts our elation,
There is a heavenly home for the righteous and persecuted nation.

Oh, there's a place, there is a place that has started in our heart!
Where praise, and worship to the righteous King will never depart!
We will sing glory, glory, glory and receive our jeweled golden crown.
For our home the kingdom of our faith, at last, we have finally found!
Through trials and tribulations, we've journeyed to our destination.
There is a heavenly home for the righteous and persecuted nation.

Fruit of the Spirit

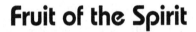

FLOW IN PEACE AND PATIENCE
RADIATE IN JOY
UPLIFT AND REWARD FAITHFULNESS
IMPART GENTLENESS AND KINDNESS
TRANSFER LOVE AND GOODNESS

Agape the Greatest Love We Know

To show Love, we don't ever need reasons,
But we remember more during special times and seasons.
Anytime is a great time to show that you Love,
When you're connected with the radiant shine from above.
Brighter than the shining midday sun aglow,
That's Agape the greatest Love we know.

It shouldn't matter what we do or what we say.
We all make many mistakes each moment and every day.
Sometimes we feel like we are all alone.
When we are by ourselves and everyone is gone.
Love's presence, stronger than the highest gust of wind to blow.
That's Agape the greatest Love we know.

True Love is unconditionally given.
It's from deep within the heart and is powerfully driven.
Sometimes we can't always express how we sincerely feel.
Time goes by and our open hearts start to reveal.
Compassion seed rains on the thirsty soul where we sow.
That's Agape the greatest Love we know.

Love grows and grows with each passing day.
Even when it's gloomy and clouds appear dark and gray.
We may not know nor always see.
The Love that God has placed between you and me.
It's intensified like the waves of the ocean's flow.
That's Agape the greatest Love we know.

It's kind of funny how we can even get mad.
Then we have to remember what God's word said.
Whatever upsets you with a heart filled fret.
Forgive, forget, to prevent the love flow blockage and painful regret.
Flaws will dim as you magnify the kind words and deeds they show.
That's Agape the greatest Love we know.

Strengthened by my God's Great Joy

When I feel the muscles of my spirit draining and getting weak,
I know it's time for nourishment and exercise that I must seek.
I feed myself with God's life-giving word.
And fight the weaknesses with its sharp cutting sword.
Especially when everything seems to easily annoy,
It's time to be strengthened by God's great joy.

Happiness not joy depends on life's situation.
But joy is a continuous movement of spiritual restoration.
Practicing always with a daily dose of positive meditation,
With the mind thinking on God's beautifully blessed creation.
Bouncing back and forth like a little child's toy.
You become fun-filled and strengthened by God's great joy.

The spiritual water that I bring to the scene,
Better than soda, or coffee with French vanilla cream.
The spiritual stream flowing irrigates each holy cell,
Guiding my spiritual muscles from dryness to an overflowing well,
Consecration is the next step that I must now employ.
Being filled and strengthened by God's great joy.

Now I must continue with a song and praise.
As I stand strong, my spirit has been raised,
I lift my strong arms and vigorously clap my hands.
With all parts active in all the system bands.
Victory is mine over weaknesses that I can now destroy.
Empowered and strengthened by God's great joy.

Peace, Peace, and Peace God's Precious Peace

On what seems to be a hot, steamy and sunny day,
The cool calming breeze gently comes by your way.
Not only cooling the body but it brings soundness to the mind.
If only for that moment you seemed to feel fine.
The hot sweltering heat immediately starts to cease.
That's peace, peace, peace, God's precious peace.

Think of sitting by the river, lake or just a small stream,
That brings a soothing comfort that feels so gentle and serene.
Visualize the steady moving tranquility of the flow,
Stirring up within you a warm, relaxing glow,
The troubles of the world you can now easily release.
That's peace, peace, peace God's precious peace.

Riding and looking at God's awesome creation,
It fills you with a positive outlook and great expectation.
When you look at the green grass and beautiful colored flowers,
It reminds you to give your worry to him and his strong powers.
Every worry and anxiousness suddenly starts to decrease.
That's peace, peace, peace God's precious peace.

God's peace is one that passes all understanding.
Working it out for you with his purpose and his planning,
Never leaving you and never forsaking you.
Always there leading and guiding you through,
You're his child one of the greatest and not the least.
That's peace, peace, peace, God's precious peace.

Patience the Fruit Wait, Wait and Wait

When things don't seem to go your way
And problems come forth day by day
Be steadfast, rejoice and try to endure.
For God is on his way for this you can be sure,
The afflictions, pressure or whatever the state.
Patience the Fruit wait, wait and wait.

Suffering and hardship produce patience even more.
A big triumph you will surely score.
Persevere, forbear, and always hold out.
The victory will be yours, and you can shout, shout, and shout.
Consecrate, be still continue to meditate.
Patience the Fruit, wait, wait, and wait.

The race is not given to the swift or the strong.
But the one who knows how to keep holding on.
Be strengthened with power from God on high.
Trust and believe he's coming by.
Strip off weight and sin as you keep an eye on the gate.
Patience the Fruit, wait, wait, and wait.

Watching and worrying will not move the clock
Remember his word and just ask to seek and knock.
For God works in time, through time and to time,
He operates through his own moment to chime.
When your seasonal time comes, his arrival will not be late.
Patience the Fruit, wait, wait, and wait.

Random Acts of Kindness

When you see a head hung down.
Burdened and bowing troubled to the ground.
Say a kind word to bring some relief.
It doesn't have to be long just lovingly brief.
You may never know how much you have blessed.
By showing a random act of kindness,

When you know, someone is hungry, and they need food.
Don't judge and be mean and say something rude.
The circumstances you may never know.
Empathy, compassion, and love you must show.
Give heartily out of the success you possess.
Reach out to others with a random act of kindness.

Sickness is something you can't always control.
It can take a toll on your body, mind, and soul.
Just a visit, call, or card can mean so much.
Like an expression from your heart from our masters' touch.
You can ease some feelings of extreme distress.
By touching them with a random act of kindness,

You can always find a way to lift someone up.
When you let the joy overflow out of your cup,
You never know when you might have a need.
So cheerfully start planting a fruitful caring seed.
Look for opportunities to pass the love test.
With many random acts of kindness.

Sowing Good Seeds along the Way

When the hearts of men begins to tearfully cry,
Your spirit will not just let you uncaringly pass them by.
The hungry now you must stop and lovingly feed.
By quickly supplying provisions for their daily need.
Your heart says give what you have without delay,
Start sowing good seeds along the way.

Nursing homes have many who are lonely, sick, and sad.
They need a song, a visit, or a hug to make them glad.
Stop and let them know that you truly and really care.
Bring a smile to an unhappy empty and blank stare.
The elderly needs us each and every day.
Begin sowing good seeds along the way.

The prison or jail you might not want to go.
But seeing the good in others compassion from you begins to flow.
They may know or may not know the merciful God from above.
You must share with them his grace and abundant love.
Let his light in you brighten their darkness with his radiant sunray.
Let us generously and freely sow good seeds along the way.

The naked and homeless stranger must be ministered to by you.
To enhance your own witness they must see you sincerely true.
Judge not some things you may see or don't quite understand.
But you do know you must do all the good while you can.
Give them a blanket, a coin and now for them you must pray.
Continue to sow good seeds along the way.

God's Everlasting and Glorious Faithfulness

From the beginning to the end God is always true.
Binding and sealing his promises on the earth for me and you.
The universal sun, moon, and stars hang by the promises that He spoke.
Earth sprinkles of rain and rainbow from the heavenly floods soak,
They magnify amazing handiwork from north, south, east, and west.
That's God's everlasting and glorious faithfulness.

God's enduring word internally written by the men of old.
They gathered all of His promises that ministers daily to our soul.
That eternal book of the covenant we must faithfully and daily read.
The perfection of wisdom and, knowledge is sown as a faithful seed.
We must live out our promises to each other and give our very best.
Just like God's everlasting and glorious faithfulness.

People may sometimes let us down, but in him, we can depend.
He secured us with his salvation when he saved us from our sin.
He promised refuge of escape from the temptations by his hand.
As God works through us with his eternal purpose and his plan,
From the soothing comfort of his breast in this promise, we can rest.
Loving and trusting in God's everlasting and glorious faithfulness.

God is the same yesterday, today and tomorrow never will he change.
Just like the seasons that we never can rearrange.
His mercies are fresh as the dew each and every day.
We can trust in him and unfailing love no matter what comes or may.
Always finding comfort in the one who blesses, bless, and blesses.
This is God's everlasting and glorious faithfulness.

Gentle Touches

A soft touch, a hug, is such a soothing embrace.
It helps you continue your journey in life's great race.
Like the feel of a fragile petal as a hand touches you,
Impacting you positively in what you think to say or do.
You begin to feel so great, healthy and grand.
From your heart, you felt someone touch with a soft, gentle hand.

The sounds of hustling and bustling seem to have no end.
Suddenly comfort comes from the sound of a rustling wind.
Your body relaxes, and you can now clearly hear.
Good morning is a peaceful musical expression to your ear.
The serene sound of birds chirping through God's vast land,
Like a steady heartbeat vibrating from the touch of a gentle hand.

Oh, taste and savor God's delicious sweetness.
Sugar glazed praises muffling the tongues of harsh bitterness.
Replaced with blessed words of encouragement and compliments,
I can taste and swallow the sweetness like dinner peppermints.
Now you can press and continue with God's perfect plan.
You can hear quiet, sweet Godly words from a heartfelt, gentle hand.

I look at the falling of each flake of snow.
Feeling soft and gentle as the wind begins to blow.
Each flake is uniquely created with God's gentle touch of grace.
I look and see smiles of all kinds glowing from each face.
They march gallantly in a rhythmic, harmonious, united band.
The unique flakes are moving calmly from the touch of a gentle hand.

With Self Control Our Flesh We Can Deny

Temperance and Discipline help the race to be won.
Like an athlete desiring victory with every run.
The beast of our tongue we must restrain.
For all it brings are heartaches and pain.
Negative thoughts and words we can forcefully defy.
With self-control our flesh we can deny.

The lust of the eye wants all that it can see.
The appetite is never satisfied for you or for me.
The pride of life covets what we see in others.
It causes envy and jealousy for our sisters and brothers.
Exalt not yourself so great on a pedestal high.
With self-control our flesh we can deny.

A negative thought can cause wrong actions to flow.
Your positive thoughts produce fruit that will grow and grow.
It will give the best peace and relaxation to a troubled mind.
With God's Spirit from heaven so calm, serene and divine.
For this kind of guiltless peace, you cannot buy.
With self-control our flesh we can deny.

The battle is not given to the swift or the strong
But he who looks up and keeps going on.
Wait on the Lord who refreshes the saint.
He can mount your wings high when you begin to feel faint.
Be victorious, don't give up, but continue to try.
With self-control our flesh we can deny.

Poetry Reflections

1. **Inspirational Affirmations**

   _____
   _____
   _____
   _____
   _____

2. **Self -Reflections (consolation, comfort, conviction, connections, etc.)**_____

   _____
   _____
   _____
   _____
   _____

3. **Scripture Reflection**_____

   _____
   _____
   _____
   _____

4. **Implementation (goal setting)**
   Self_____

   _____
   _____
   _____
   _____

   Others_____

   _____
   _____
   _____
   _____

   Prayer of Thanksgiving & Praise_____

   _____
   _____
   _____
   _____

Emotional
ENCOURAGERS

HE HEALS THE BROKEN HEARTED
AND BANDAGES THEIR WOUNDS
PSALMS 147:3 (GNTD)

Emotional Encouragement Word Message

ENCOURAGE YOURSELF

MAGNIFY THE LORD AND MEDITATE

OPTIMISM IS HEALING

THINK POSITIVE AND PRAY

IMPROVISE WHEN NECESSARY

ORGANIZE

NEGATIVITY SHOULD BE AVOIDED

SEEK SPIRITUAL SUPPORT SYSTEMS

No More Storms and No More Rain

Our love one worshiped, sang and gave God the Praise.
She ran hard and finished her race.
Though she might have gotten tired weary and worn,
She finished the purpose and plan for which she was born,
It was time for her to go and leave the loved ones who remain.
No more Storm and no more rain.

Some seasons are short, and some are long.
When spring comes, winter is gone.
Time does not consider the quantity nor size.
But the one who endures, God still gives their prize.
She ran and slowed as she felt her body drain.
No more Storm and no more rain.

Family and friends took a seat with her on the ride,
As she journeyed peacefully to the other side,
Even though she needed your show of kindness and Love,
She felt the exhilarating comfort from her God above.
She glanced out and saw through her traveling train.
No more Storm, and no more rain.

Cover, teach and protect the child she left behind.
As you did with her, so God she could find.
She knew the Love each of you would share.
And found comfort in knowing that you would be there.
Let her little child know she's with the God who took her pain.
No more Storm and nor more rain.

Now when you think of seven.
Think of her completion and move to Heaven.
Past the sunshine so brilliantly bright.
Now a part of the Illuminous and Glorious Light.
With loved ones and Jesus Christ who paid the price for her eternal gain.
No more Storm and no more rain.

Life's Journey Has a Beginning and an End

Life's journey may be short or long.
It's like a vapor, we're here then we're gone.
Sometimes life stops us right in our track.
And reminds us to dust we must go back.
Sometimes we break, and we may bend
Life's journey has a beginning and an end.

But there's one sure thing about the life we know.
What really lasts forever is the love we show.
During life's journey, if we're giving out love.
That's something we know that comes from above.
Love helps our broken hearts to mend.
Life's journey has a beginning and an end.

So keep the good memories forever in your mind.
And stir up the love seeds that were left behind.
So weep, cry and mourn if you must.
But for joy and strength, in God, you can trust.
After sadness, change comes to your face with a grin,
Life's journey has a beginning and an end.

Be strong in the lord in the Spirit of his might.
Tears might come in the darkest of the night.
But in the morn, the sun will surely shine.
And now you smile, and you begin to feel fine.
God's joy he gives and does not lend.
Life's journey has a beginning and an end.

We Will Truly Miss You

God has showered us with blessings from heaven above.
Full of a heart of care and Agape love,
You were a breeze of fresh air fragrant and new.
From our hearts of **Love**, we will truly miss you.

As we think of your presence and our abundant loss,
It's our hope that as God guides, our paths will cross.
The face of our countenance was solemn and blue,
From our hearts of **Love,** we will truly miss you.

Even though there were things that were not understood,
You continued to work as much as you could.
The more we worked together our communication grew.
From our hearts of **Love**, we will truly miss you.

As the righteousness of God's Glory began to shine,
I'm happy that you were no longer left blind,
You could see us with spiritual eyes discerning and true.
From our hearts of **Love**, we will truly miss you.

I know you must have given it your very best try.
And cried to the Lord, must I stay and ask why.
To God's will, you yielded as you thought it through and through.
From our hearts of **Love,** we will truly miss you.

Our hearts are teary with a groan and a cry.
For we didn't get to say to you goodbye,
We'll delight in our memories as a beautiful mountain view.
From our hearts of **Love**, we will truly miss you.

Sometime in the distant future on some glorious day,
God's path may lead each of you joyfully back this way.
So maybe not goodbye forever, we'll see what the Spirit will do.
From our hearts of **Love,** we will truly miss you

A Reflection of Deceased Last Days

I Had to Go
You were right there near when I got to the very end.
That's what I call a fellow Christian, family and a friend.
Some of you couldn't physically be there,
But I knew the church and others were interceding in prayer.
I felt everyone's love when your caring started to flow.
But it was time, and I knew that I had to go.

I knew my house was in order and I was ready to leave.
My body was weak and tired, and my mission had been achieved.
I had been going through suffering for oh so long.
But my spirit day by day had begun to grow strong.
I got on the old ship of Zion, and it started to row.
For it was time, and I knew that I had to go,

While operating in God's divine and heavenly will,
I surrendered all, and my body began to yield.
There were some leaks in this building, and I had to move on.
Especially with what the revelation light had shown.
Family, friends and I were together at home.
And on their smiling face was a youthful glow
And I knew then that it was time for me to go.

So I'm fine now and doing oh so well.
It's even better than anything any story could tell.
I feel so fresh energetic and renewed.
It's more beautiful than any landscape that we've ever viewed.
Even though you will miss me and this I know.
But it was time, and I inevitably had to go.

Love in Action (Thank you)

No one had to beg cry, petition or plead.
By taking the love route, you began to lead.
You couldn't pass by and say there's nothing I can do.
Because the Love of God was inside of you,
Though the need might be, sickness, death or emotional pain.
The heart of compassion flowed, from Christ, through your vein.
With your Love in Action, we can honestly say.
Thank you, thank you, for your Love this day.

The language of Love is not just what you say.
It's what you do without looking for pay.
You have not just loved in word or in speech,
Souls of suffering you would not be able to reach.
But you moved according to God's word or deed in truth,
For those you saw in despair, sick or destitute.
The voice of your heart spoke, and you moved without delay.
With Love in Action Thank you, from within my heart I pray.

You listened from within, and you carefully start to look.
As you thought of works, God had shown you, in his most influential book.
Searching and seeking for your resources, your talent, and gift.
To be used to give God's hurting child, a kind and encouraging lift.
God has given each one of us something special for you and me.
It may be cooking, cleaning, exhorting or singing a melody.
With Love in Action, you've always been there.
Thank you for your cards, calls, or visits and showing that you care.

As a willing considerate vessel, God's grace flows to you from above.
To show you, his greatest gift, and his sacrificial Love,
Wait on the Lord, for he will surely and freely bless.
Your reward will be bountiful and magnificent, for you've passed a love test.
The work you've done as a servant, he has seen, and he has known.
He will reward you openly as you reap what you have sown.
So your Love in Action has not been in vain.
We Thank You, We Thank You, for soothing our pain.

Now let's praise God together for what he has done!
For out of his great Love he gave us his son.
Love is not Love until you give it away.
Therefore we bow unto God in submission as we pray.
We give a great Hallelujah for his Love and sacrifice!
It wasn't because we were so good, so pleasant, or nice.
His Love in Action makes us shout, dance, and sing!
I say Thank You for being a servant of our Lord the beloved King.

A Memorial Salute of Love for Mom and Dad

A father and a mother are like none other.
We now find comfort in our love for one another.
The family always pulled together in God's strength and might,
Now we're living out what they taught us about wrong and right.
It did not require them to be a college grad.
So we salute our love to our mom and dad.

They had difficulties with life's troubles and pain.
But it taught us how to overcome the storm and the rain.
We learned that our help comes from high above the hill.
Where we receive comfort from God's word revealed.
We remember the designated time we had to go to bed.
For that, we salute with love our mom and our dad.

As we leave, depart, and we each go our different way.
Always remembering church on Sunday was our special day.
Their journey here has now come to an end.
A new life for them will begin, and for that, on our knees, we bend.
Respect, compassion, and helping others were put in our head.
We now lovingly salute our Mom and our Dad.

We're thankful that they loved God, the Father above.
They never lost sight of the divine Agape love.
So now we can let them serenely rest in peace.
For they are only asleep and not deceased,
By the guidance of the Holy Spirit, they were led.
A high lovingly salute we give to our mom and our dad.

Memories of Christmas Past

Christmas this year might bring to you a tear.
There's something deep within that you can always hold dear.
They are precious Memories of Christmas Past.
That can never leave you but will always last
For deep down in the depths of your heart,
Find loving memories that should never depart.

The anguish and despair can bring you great pain.
Like clouds of hurt, that comes down like rain.
The mind, that's illuminated by God's great light.
Can for this Christmas shine a little bright.
For those Memories of Christmas Past,
They can flash in your mind ever so fast.

What's in your heart and mind you carry each day,
You have a God, who can show you the way.
Jesus has been here and he is now bodily gone,
The passion in your soul says he has not left you alone.
Memories of Christmas Past If only for a moment fleeting,
Like a new heart with a restored steady beating.

As Christmas comes closer for you this year,
Remember that your loved one is ever so near.
As close as the breathing of the days' fresh air,
You can't see it but you know that it's there.
In your heart and in your renewed mind,
Memories of Christmas Past you will find.

Find a picture or a symbol and put it on the tree.
As you pass by, fall down on your knee.
Give God the Praise for what he has given you.
In memorial say "What can I, now also do too?"
With heartfelt Memories from Christmas Past,
Peaceful life anew will become present at last.

Focusing in Stressful Times

Focus your camera with a believing faithful film
Your focus shouldn't be clouded nor should it be dim.
Look very close and seek your background place.
Stare with fixation until you find a trusting face.
Your direction should be in the brightest of light.
Until you focus and see Christ shining so bright.

Listen for the voice that says, "Are you ready, I'm right here.
Suddenly you realize he is ever so near.
Now snap the picture and place it in your heart.
And know that in the darkest of times, he shall never depart.
Life's many distractions will always be there.
But be in peace knowing you'll find his face everywhere.

So when the storms of life began to embark,
Stay focused and move with the light he has sparked.
There are times that you might stumble and you might fall.
Keep going bit by bit even if you have to crawl.
Forever keeping your eyes on the highest prize,
Because you know God's strength will help you rise.

Now develop your film with a prayer and praise.
Watch it become clearer the higher it's raised.
He's high and lifted up front, back and right by your side.
Leading you through the storm with the spirit as your guide,
Remembering not by strength nor by might,
The almighty God has already won the fight.

Be of Good Cheer

I will place on God's alter what I cannot fix.
It will not be allowed to make me anxious or sick.
I will smile with laughter and decrease stress.
Listening to melodious music and bringing my mind to rest.
Knowing that my God cares and is always near,
As I think of this, I will be of good cheer.

Seeking and searching I will find my release.
Allowing the tension, stress, and anxiety to slowly decrease,
As my body and mind relax and gradually feels better at last.
Basking at this moment, I will put my worries in the past.
Trusting and having faith I will overcome my deepest fear.
While meditating on the present, I will be of good cheer.

I will think about the plans and dreams that are deep in my heart.
Focusing on these thoughts only as I look for where to start,
By tearing away the baggage that I've carried so long,
Optimism will master my heartaches and pain so that I can grow strong.
Replacing sadness with chuckles and smiles in place of each tear,
As I move toward my dreams, I will be of good cheer.

Many, many blessings have come and will continue my way.
For this, I will give thanks and not procrastinate or delay.
Because God has been so very good to me,
Blinded by stress, I sometimes failed to look and see.
The treasures in my heart are now so dear and clear.
For each of my blessings, I will be of good cheer.

Solace from Mother's Memory Lane

Special days are sometimes full of grief and oh so hard.
When we think of the mothers, who had to depart,
The tears seem to stream in a steady flow.
My deep hurting emotions I try not to show.
Trying to find ways to ease the hurt and the pain,
I seek solace from my mother's memory lane.

I start to remember from the heart all of her love.
Believing it is strong enough to last from above.
Soaking in my mind is all of her loving care,
The hearts are torn and tattered; I now seem able to bear.
The hurt slowly moves through the clogs of the drain.
I find solace from mother's memory lane.

I know God's timing is what it's going to take.
She would want me to move on for my own sake.
Emotional healing will soon come day by day.
Trusting in God will help me find my way.
Even with my loss mom's strength is my gain.
I find solace from mother's memory lane.

She taught me that during struggles we should always pray.
In every situation that comes when things are cloudy and gray.
Remembering worship songs the choir would always sing,
My mind relaxes from the musical sounds they bring.
The sunshine always comes after the clouds and the rain.
I found solace from the mother's memory lane.

Faith Overcomes Frustration and Anxious Fear

Memorize and speak scriptures with a faith fulfilling word.
They will swiftly move as a sharp cutting two edge sword.
Train your mind to focus on the language of light not sight.
Dispel the fearful darkness with dominant faith and might.
Trust and believe that God's protective presence is always near.
Faith overcomes frustration and anxious fear.

Face your fears and trust the word that God gave.
Greater is he that is in you, so now stand up tall and be brave.
Your imagination creates and magnifies the seen and unseen.
Making it appear scary even when it's peaceful and serene.
Find a distraction about something held near and dear.
Faith overcomes frustration and anxious fear.

Your faith can get you through the darkest time of night.
And take away your phobia, anxiousness, and fright.
Think of relaxing and pleasant things that you love to do.
The hardest times you will be able to get through.
Distresses and limitations should not always bring a tear.
Faith overcomes frustration and anxious fear.

Fear comes from the enemy to make you sad and blue.
The problems and difficulties may never happen to you.
Think calmly when distress and panic come your way.
Be strong in the Lord and cast in the sea your dismal dismay.
Power of the spoken tongue will create a peaceful atmosphere.
Faith overcomes frustration and anxious fear.

Soar Above Being Victimized Controlled and Abused

God has lifted and brought you safely alive and out,
Give him your most loud, passionate and thankful shout.
Ahead of you, there is something spectacular and great!
Let not this past tragedy decide your present and your fate.
Though you were mistreated physically and emotionally misused,
Soar above being victimized controlled and abused.

You are more powerful now and internally strong.
Don't allow the perpetrator to victimize and bound you in his wrong.
Overcome and let not your self be gripped by guilt and shame.
You are not the one to receive and carry the blame.
Be a conqueror of the talk and reject the path of the accused.
Soar above being victimized controlled and abused.

Don't pick your wounds until they fester and bleed.
Allow God's word in your heart to plant a soothing seed.
Leave the scab on it so that it can begin to heal.
Through his strength, you must yield, and you must kneel.
Read the bible daily and shout the good news.
Soar above being victimized controlled and abused.

You are wonderfully and beautifully made.
Even though you were violated and betrayed,
Resist disgust and let God clothe you with loving self-esteem
He can restore your eyes sparkling with a bright gleam.
Your vibrant light will now shine with a new charged fuse.
Soar high above being victimized controlled and abused.

Poetry Reflections

1. **Inspirational Affirmations**

   _____
   _____
   _____
   _____
   _____

2. **Self -Reflections (consolation, comfort, conviction, connections, etc.)_____**

   _____
   _____
   _____
   _____
   _____

3. **Scripture Reflection_____**

   _____
   _____
   _____
   _____
   _____

4. **Implementation (goal setting)**
   Self_____

   _____
   _____
   _____
   _____

   Others_____

   _____
   _____
   _____
   _____

   Prayer of Thanksgiving & Praise_____

   _____
   _____
   _____
   _____

Motivational
ENCOURAGERS

Finally brothers and sisters whatever is true, whatever is noble, whatever is right, whatever is pure, whatever is lovely, whatever is admirable- if anything is excellent or praiseworthy - think about such things.
Phillippians 4:8 NIV

Motivation Word Message

MOMENTS OF MEDITATION MEANS MUCH
OBSTACLES ARE CHALLENGES
TASK COMMIT TO THE FINISH LINE
IMPROVE ONE STEP AT A TIME
VISUALIZE YOUR GOALS
APPOINT TALENTED PEOPLE
TRY!   TRY!   TRY!
IMAGINE IMPOSSIBILITIES BECOMING POSSIBLE
OPPORTUNITY PROVIDES DOORS TO OPEN
NEVER GIVE UP

Look Unto the Hills Way Above the Sky

Be still and know that God is near.
Even, when we have to shed a tear,
As we ease away our sorrow shows,
God's ever-present and he always knows.
The purpose, the plan and even the why,
So look to the hills, way above the sky.

When our body wracks with so much pain,
It's like a never-ending storm and rain.
When it seems like we can't take much more,
The tide has moved in upon the distant shore,
With a high pitched wail, we might begin to cry
Then look to the hills, way above the sky.

The body seems to suffer for oh so long.
But day by day the spirit grows strong.
Each day seems to bring new hopes of light.
As you look at the daily sun shining so bright,
You listen to the birds sing as they begin to fly.
And look to the hills, way above the sky.

Sing your song and meditate each day.
On the good, and the best that has come your way.
Count all the blessings and battles you've won.
Knowing God will complete what he has begun.
This shall pass as you persevere and try,
Look unto the hills way above the sky.

Don't give up and don't give in.
Adversity has not and will never win.
For friends and loved ones caring smiles,
It will carry you further miles and miles.
Take comfort in knowing that you can fly.
Look to the hills way above the sky.

The love, the joy, and the peace you seek,
Can come quickly when you feel ever so weak,
Praise and praise when you feel the distress,
God's peace can help you sleep, slumber and rest.
He looks low, brings comfort, and sits ever so high.
Always look to the hills way above the sky.

Be Encouraged you're Never Left Alone

Sometimes you feel so down and out.
Until all you want to do is cry and shout.
You're in a crowd but you feel all by yourself.
As if everybody's gone, and you're the only one that's left.
So don't just sit with tears and a moan.
Be encouraged you're never left alone.

Sometimes the wind might blow with the storm and the rain.
Just remember to try not to complain.
Stir good memories and bring calm to the wind.
The good thoughts will bring happiness with a smile and a grin.
Clouds will dispel and the light will be shown.
Be encouraged you're never left alone.

Don't toss and turn with a sleepless night.
God does not leave you alone with the battle to fight.
Prayer and the word are tools you can use.
They're like a balm in Gilead to soothe life's bruise.
He'll never leave you comfortless and all on your own.
Be encouraged you're never left alone.

Everybody has something they must go through.
Relatives, friends, and neighbors as well as you,
But there's a God in spirit within you every day.
When your days are gray just call on him and pray.
Look above the mountain tops for he's high upon the throne.
Be encouraged you're never left alone

Power over Sin as We Struggle Within

The spirit is willing but the flesh is weak.
Therefore, Jesus Christ is who we should seek.
Only from him can we get the strength that we need.
The battle we can conquer with victory and succeed.
We're torn and worn but the Holy Spirit will mend.
We have power over sin as we struggle within.

Fight the lust of the eye, and the lust of the flesh.
With God's word there is daily refresh.
Slowly creeping in us is the pride of life.
Seeking to cut soul and spirit with a searing knife,
But there is no way we cannot win.
We have power over sin as we struggle within.

Victory is ours so don't give up just persevere.
Knowing that the help we need is ever so near.
The world bows down to the greatness in us.
For it's in God's power that we have our trust.
He has already won the battle over satan and sin.
We have power over sin as we struggle within.

The shedding of the Lord's blood was not in vain.
Nor was his sweat, suffering and his great pain,
For there is dynamite power in the Lamb's blood,
It has come to wash us with an overwhelming flood.
With the repentance of change we start all over again.
Because we have power over sin as we struggle within.

Just Give to God Your Heavy Load

When you feel broken into small pieces bit by bit
And nothing comes together as you ponder and sit.
Talk to Jesus he's near and very close by.
He knows the, who's, what's, and even the why.
Even a chirping bird has a calming story to be told.
Just give God your heavy load.

You were once just a baby with a life of ease.
Nothing to worry about always being pleased,
But now you don't seem to know which way to go.
Like that crawling baby, others seem to move oh so slow.
You're never left alone or out in the cold.
Always give God your heavy load.

Don't forget to let others know that you have a need.
Just share and communicate you don't have to plead.
You just follow the leaders God has divinely sent your way.
They've seen the burdens on your face as sad, cloudy and gray.
They too will need help when they travel the same bumpy road.
Always give God your heavy load.

Weights are meant to be carried by many coming together.
Making the load feel as light as a fluttering feather.
The Lord can put back the pieces no matter how small.
Just be patient whether you're a baby or grown he's heard your call.
In the dark tunnels of life, his guiding light will unfold.
Remember give God your heavy load.

Don't give up on the Abundant Life

Abundant life is more than just making a living.
It's about love, joy, longsuffering, and giving.
Living consist of jobs, money, and material things,
Small things lift our spirit, and with a song, our voice sings.
We often see adversity and tragedies, and strife.
But don't give up on the abundant life.

Don't look around to see what you need.
But find inside you God's planted seed.
With abilities, gifts, and talents unique only to you,
Glorify God's creation and to yourself be true.
Enjoy times with family, husband, or wife.
But don't give up on the abundant life.

All you need is faith in God to succeed.
It's not intertwined with hustle, bustle, and greed.
Living in this world can throw you a curve.
But life's blessings can ease pressure on your nerve.
The pain is cut with the word of God's sharp, smooth knife.
You can't give up on the abundant life.

God has given you the sunshine and the rain.
With patience the flowers and green grass you will gain,
You can pull through being thankful for God's purpose and plan.
With peace knowing that in his hand it will be great and grand.
Amid the darkness, disappointment, and strife,
Don't give up on the abundant life.

Cast Every Care
Proverbs 3:56

When you're working, relaxing and feeling fine,
Everything thing seems well with the body and the mind.
All of a sudden you don't feel quite right.
Your footsteps are shaky, and your head feels light.
The sickness came quickly it seems from nowhere
Your spirit says now you must cast every care.

You know immediately that something is wrong.
Your body doesn't feel well, alert or strong.
Thinking the worst your heart begins to sink
To stay healthy, positive thoughts you must think.
For this trial, your spiritual mind will prepare.
Faith now says you must cast every care.

You're hoping with the medicine you'll get better quick.
But after a while, you're still feeling sick.
You do what you can to make it go away
But things remain the same from day to day.
The doctor is the next place you must go,
Hoping he will not tell you what you don't want to know

You wonder and ponder as to what he will say.
Moving slowly trying hard to create a delay
When you arrive and sit for just a little a while.
You wonder to yourself if this is the last mile.
You notice a Bible sitting on the table,
Knowing you will find the truth and not just a fable.

Your burden becomes lighter as you pick up the book.
Everything seems brighter as you begin to look.
It says trust in God whatever the circumstance might be.
Your heart leaps with joy, happiness, and glee!
Believing whatever the diagnosis, you surely can bear.
Because your faith says to you cast your every care.

Even though doubt may sometimes come your way,
Sunshine will peep through the clouds that appear to be gray.
All of your dedicated faith walks will eventually kick in,
God's strength will give you the victory, and you will surely win.
The sunshine will illuminate brightly as it brings forth a glare.
For in God you have trusted to cast your every care.

A New Season is coming in Your Life

Changes come from time to time, during a time and in time.
God's creation shows us many varieties of another kind.
Summer, Winter-Spring, and Fall,
Each in its time stands strong and tall,
Sometimes joy, happiness, pain or strife,
There's a new season coming in your life.

At the end of summer, the leaves must fall.
But it brings an array of colors that's a beauty for us all.
Even the temperature has it's time to change,
Slowly changing to a more cooling range,
We quickly adapt as a man toward a lovely wife.
There's a new season coming in your life.

Then comes the season that we sometimes dread,
With the cold, the sleet and the snow widespread,
Like our sickness, pain, despair, and distress.
We accommodate the temporary to avoid stress.
Fret not the cold and the ice but trust God with all your might.
There's a new season coming in your life.

The physical is temporary, and it is not here to stay.
Gone is the past the future will bring a new day.
You know your change will come if you just hang on,
The bitter and the sweet only made you strong.
Even though your heart, may have been cut with a sharp knife.
There's a new season coming in your life.

Make A Place of Contentment and Stillness and Peace

Conflict with self and others can come with any relationship.
We must know how to be quiet and zip our tongue and lip.
Just being a peaceful person is not ever nearly enough.
We have to know how to help others when things get rough and tough.
Helping life's frustrations, and high flying emotions to decrease,
Let's make a place of contentment and stillness and peace.

Being a problem solver is always the best way to go.
Stop tempers from flaring, and quiet the intense storms that blow.
Learn how to say peace be still to an aggressive situation.
And calmly use God-given skills as solutions to mediation.
We can cause turmoil, strife, and winds of conflict to cease.
Let's make a place of contentment and stillness and peace.

Sometimes things can quickly get wild.
Consult your father's way because you're still his child.
Bring others together and begin a time to pray.
Serenity will begin to come in its own calm and unique way.
Like a caged dove finding his freedom of release.
Let's make a place of contentment and stillness and peace.

Share the peace within that you've found for yourself.
Be sure to include others making sure they are not left.
In Jesus, you've found the peace that everyone needs.
Thank God you know how to plant peaceful mind seeds.
Thoughts from God's word will help tranquility to increase.
Let's make a place of contentment and stillness and peace.

Help One Another

Stop! Slow down, my sister and my brother.
It's time for us to help one another.
We just can't walk and pass on by.
For within each other we must desire to try.
I need you, and you need me.
We can work hand in hand for the world to see.

We're all moving at such a fast pace.
It's like we're running in a track and field race.
Everybody's busy doing their own thing.
They can't hear the emergency bell ring.
Until something happens at their own back door,
Then it's like the loud sound of a lion's roar.

Trouble is coming from here and there.
Not just one place but from everywhere.
If it's not one thing, it's another.
So let's pitch in and help each other.
You do your part, and I'll do mine.
For we're both offering something of a different kind.

Let's walk hand in hand empowered together,
We can make this world much, much better.
Letting others know they're not in this alone.
Love and empathy have not yet gone.
Our eyes are open, and now we see the need.
Slowing down and stopping to do our good deed.

Believe God He Answers So Just Wait

Sometimes it seems that things take so long.
And everything appears to always go wrong.
You can't see the daylight from the darkness.
Then you wonder if this is only a test for my best.
Will you pass or fail and walk through the faith gate.
Or believe God, he answers so just wait.

You look to God and you just pray and you pray.
Then you wonder if this a no, or just a delay.
Doubt emerges in your mind and faith seems gone.
But something deep inside keeps saying, hold on, hold strong.
Everything has a purpose and plan and not just a man's fate.
So believe God, he answers so just wait.

You get impatient and try to take things in your own hand.
You're only interrupting and interfering with God's plan.
Just hold on knowing and trusting that you will grow strong.
Because God never ever fails, make a mistake or go wrong.
Therefore stop, think and on God's divine word meditate.
And believe God, he answers so just wait.

All of a sudden a bright light begins to shine.
In your heart, a kindle of faith says it's going to be just fine.
You feel the warmth of his presence and begin to smile.
Now you know that all of this time was well worthwhile.
You see the plan worked for you to walk through the gate.
Believe God, he answers, so just wait.

Time to Celebrate

Time moves and goes by and speeds by oh so quick.
Just like you're well one moment and then you're sick.
Celebrate each day even if means doing something small.
It's always better than doing nothing at all.
Do special considerate acts promoting love and not hate.
So stop take some time today and happily celebrate.

Don't put off tomorrow what help can easily be done today.
Whether it's a smile, touch, or a compliment you need to say.
You're a part of a glorious plan, purpose, and design.
Listen, follow, and act with positive thoughts from your mind.
When you do so you will be glad you didn't wait.
So stop take time today and celebrate.

Listen to the melody as the chirping bird sings.
With a cheer for your heart that this day brings.
Look at the sun shining on the morning dew.
Grateful that this day is fresh and brand new,
Today with high expectations you can anticipate.
So stop and take the time today and celebrate.

Whatever state you seem to find yourself in,
Claim your victory and see yourself as a win, win, win.
Keep an attitude full of gratitude and gratefulness.
As you look around and see how well you have been blessed.
On all of these things think on and meditate.
So stop take time today and celebrate.

A New Beginning is Now in Sight

Old things will one day eventually leave disappear and past.
Even though it seems to be cemented in our lives to forever last.
We see and know that some things will come to an end.
You made it without a fall, just a slump and a bend.
There were struggles along the way and battles to fight.
But a new beginning is now in sight

There is always going to dawn a bright sunshiny day,
That leads to a radiant, luminous light guiding your way.
The darkness clouded around you with seemingly no way out.
Bringing anxiety and depression making you cry out with a shout.
Oh how precious it is to now see an end to the darkness of night.
A new beginning is now in sight.

A heaviness of guilt came when you did something wrong.
You couldn't shake off the weight for the burden was strong.
God's hidden word came swiftly to your confused, disturbed mind.
Dispelling the darkness and now you are no longer blind.
Just a glimpse at the end you could see a dim light.
A new beginning is now in sight.

Now you can keep walking toward something better and bright.
God's word has enlightened you with strength, valor and might.
His light shines brighter when in midnight the darkest of dark.
The sunrays of truth always bring days ignited with a spark.
Now cling to his promises with a grip of faith firm and tight.
A new beginning is now in sight

Seek and Find Rest to Renew Your Soul

Everything in life will eventually begin to wear and tear.
Some people find it easy to accept and to bear.
This is not a well -kept secret hidden denying others to know.
Discard worry and discontent making your boat hard to row.
They have wisely learned to whom to give complete control.
Seek and find rest to renew your soul.

Blow out negativity and breathe in goodness.
Visualize and say God is good and I am blessed.
When rejection comes, and you feel blue,
Just remember Jesus never leaves nor forsake you.
So bask in his warmth when your heart feels cold.
Seek and find rest to renew your soul.

Find your place of solace and just sit still.
To see if your temporary failure is part of a divine will.
You just might view something better coming your way.
This too shall pass so move toward a brand new day.
Relax, release and visualize your hopes and goal.
Seek and find rest to renew your soul.

Start your day with an affirmation, prayer and a smile.
Laugh and be thankful that you are still alive.
Don't rush but with leisurely ease take your time.
And the rest of the day will refreshingly go just fine.
Problems from yesterday to the Lord you have told.
Seek and find rest to renew your soul.

Poetry Reflections

1. **Inspirational Affirmations**

   _____
   _____
   _____
   _____
   _____

2. **Self -Reflections (consolation, comfort, conviction, connections, etc.)**_____

   _____
   _____
   _____
   _____
   _____

3. **Scripture Reflection**_____

   _____
   _____
   _____
   _____

4. **Implementation (goal setting)**
   Self_____

   _____
   _____
   _____
   _____

   Others_____

   _____
   _____
   _____
   _____

   Prayer of Thanksgiving & Praise_____

   _____
   _____
   _____
   _____

Christian Education
ENCOURAGERS

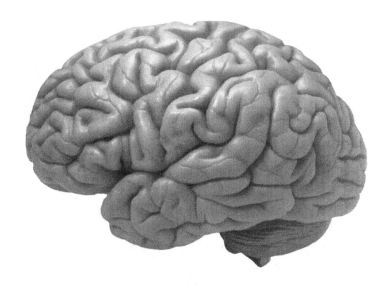

Study to show thyself approved unto God,
a workman that needed not be ashamed
rightly dividing the word of truth.
2 Timothy 2:15 KJV

Christian Education Word Message

EXPLORE EXECUTE & EXPECT EXCELLENCE
DEDICATE AND DEVELOP ABILITIES
UNDERSTAND AND UTILIZE TIME WISELY
COMMIT CONCENTRATE & BE CONSISTENT
ADMIT MISTAKES AND SEEK CORRECTIONS
TACKLE THE TOUGH QUESTIONS
INCREASE BIBLICAL INFORMATION
ORGANIZE AND PRAYERFULLY PREPARE
NURTURE MENTALLY SPIRITUAL MEAT

Sunday School & Bible Study Has a Good Learning Tool

When Life knocks us against the wall,
We wonder how some people still stand tall.
They don't seem to quirk or to quiver.
But remain as peaceful as a calm flowing river.
When you are anxious and don't know where to turn just keep cool
Sunday school and Bible Study is a good working tool.

It's not the biggest secret ever kept.
It's not because they have never wept.
It's because of the knowledge of the word abound.
It's in Sunday school the password they have found.
The name of Jesus teaches a lifelong rule.
Sunday school and Bible Study is a good working tool.

This password can open knowledge doors to understanding.
With many sites that give strength to those withstanding.
Without googling you get the wisdom to perform applications,
Taking you through life's many tragic situations,
Some things can't be found on social media's website pool.
Sunday school and Bible Study is a good working tool.

The learned word talks about the peace that passes understanding.
That gives you the strength to keep on standing.
What you don't know you can always ask.
You gain help to handle life's great task.
It's like diving with the Holy Spirits fiery fuel.
Sunday school and Bible Study is a good working tool.

So walk with haste to the knowledge door.
To grow, mature and with others, you'll soar.
Ever reading, learning and steadily growing.
With God's wisdom continuously glowing.
Satan's darts of confusion you're not easily fooled.
Sunday school and Bible Study is a good working tool.

Sunday School Is the Place for Me

I want to learn, and I want to grow.
So there are some things I must know.
The Bible's truth is the best knowledge tree.
Therefore Sunday School is the place for me.

While seeking God and his particular way,
Even the disciples had to learn how to pray.
Teachers are there to help us see.
That Sunday School is the place for me.

Study to show approval unto our God above,
To know and understand more about the Lord we love,
God's knowledge doesn't require a Ph.D. degree.
Only Sunday School which is the place for me.

In his school of the word, there is no pass or fail,
But light and lamp keeping me on the right trail,
Asking and sharing with Saints who are free.
Makes Sunday School the place for me.

Now I can grow and become spiritually strong.
God's word teaches me the right from the wrong.
I'll praise God with joyful glee.
Because Sunday School is the place for me.

Job Well Done We Thank You

Teaching with Love is what you show.
As a result, students can grow, grow, and grow.
Christian Education is needed to make a good life each day.
With the Spirit's guidance, you can show them the way.
We can tell that you teach and live what you do.
So we sincerely say job well done we thank you.

Your face glows with a bright kindness light.
You brought the word with exuberance to delight.
By studying you have shown what you know,
One day you will begin to reap what you sow.
You say God's word is always enlightening and true.
So to you, we say job well done we thank you.

In you the Christ we can see,
We also come from the Christ family tree.
To plant an excellent productive seed,
You have the degree that every Christian need.
With humility, you have shared what you knew.
So we say to you well done we thank you.

Your character is evident that you have a qualified B.A.
Whenever you teach, we hear the anointing in what you say.
It didn't cost a dime your Born Again credentials were free.
We believe that for us you pray and stayed on your knee.
Binding knowledge and wisdom with an adhesive glue.
So we say job well done we thank you.

Learning is Earning for Success

It's time to start a booming dynamite new school year.
The blast off time is quickly coming and it's very near.
You must prepare, read and review year round.
You've got a glowing future for which you are bound
Put commitment in your heart and do your best.
You are learning and earning to be a success.

Your success this year is up to you.
Teachers and school staff will teach you what to do.
They'll do their part and you will do your part.
Expect and look forward to a good school start.
Commit, work and study to pass the test.
You are learning and earning to be a success.

Ignore or report the bully you see.
It's just something in you they want to be.
Remember you have a mission and a goal.
Use the life skills learned and stand up and be bold.
Don't be scared or timid when dealing with a pest.
You are learning and earning to be a success.

There's a time to work and a time for play.
Remember the difference each and every day.
Your working station is in the class.
Be among the first and not among the last.
Classroom clowns play and have fun at their desk.
But you are learning and earning to be a success.

Help Our Kids by Guiding them from the Heart

Thanks, you can help by doing what is right,
By giving to our kids God's knowledge of light,
Your talents and gifts to them you can share.
Letting them know that you truly care.
All they need is a great stepping start.
Help our kids by guiding them from the heart.

Churches may not be the most perfect place,
But the love we have is given by God's grace.
That place in heaven you will one day find.
Then and only then will you have the perfect design.
So take them to a place where they can play a part.
Help our kids by guiding them from the heart.

So strive and teach toward that ultimate perfection,
As we work to meet God's, great expectation.
With your kids and our kids learning together,
We'll help them grow in storms and sunshiny weather.
Love, kindness, and compassion overrides smart.
Help our kids by guiding them from the heart.

Let the spirit lead and guide you as you pray today.
Hopefully, the path will bring you toward a kid's way.
Boys need help with a Godly man's thrust.
So we'll put our hope in the God whom we trust.
Love will continue to work out of the seed you impart.
Help our kids by guiding them from the heart.

The Master Teacher Can Help Us Succeed

Jesus taught his disciples three and a half years.
He knew knowledge could cast away all of their fears.
He consistently taught principles by precepts and examples.
Imparting his word through stories of simple lesson samples,
God's divine knowledge always supplies what we need.
The master teacher can help us succeed.

He taught with authority the bountiful treasures he knew.
His word separated falsehood from what was really true.
For us to mature spiritually and continue to grow,
The Bible's light of instruction teaches us what we know.
The bread of life we must daily read.
The master teacher can help us succeed.

The best lesson taught is a daily Godly, and spiritual walk.
And not just from what we say with fancy powerless talk.
The Holy Spirit teachings radiating from within us we give.
Shown by the righteous life of Christ we sincerely strive to live.
Our light will direct others as we teach and we lead.
The master teacher can help us succeed.

We must study to be a workman that bears no shame.
Never seeking pious gain or a claim of prestigious fame,
The omniscient Jesus has paved the path and directed the way,
To bring men out of darkness to the enlightened knowledge of the day.
And not be tossed by every wave of doctrine but grounded in our creed.
The master teacher can help us succeed.

Praise And Worship is good, but You Need More

We love to worship and give God praise.
The power of his presence never ceases to amaze.
But when the storms of life begin to rage,
You need a class to go through God's Bible page.
And into your mind, God's knowledge should pour.
Praise and worship are good, but you need more.

The world is certainly full of our lives ups and down.
God's foundation in his word can be found.
The word can cause the enemy and his fiery darts to flee.
You will learn through studying to declare and decree.
You will thank the Lord and on your knees hit the floor.
Praise and worship are good, but you need more.

It's like the food you eat each and every day.
Taking bite by bite several times without delay,
It helps your body stay healthy, young and strong.
Your soul needs the same to help you do right not wrong.
God's word is exciting and never a bore.
Praise and worship are good, but you need more.

Therefore Sunday school and Bible study is a must.
It lifts your spiritual growth like a wind gust.
You can't stay a baby you have to spiritually grow.
Maturing in God's word with the more you know.
Get as full as you can with an abundant galore.
Praise and worship are good, but you need more.

Study the Word It's Your Guiding Light

Trouble can come your way, and you don't know what to do.
Where is a relief for the mind and spirit within you?
You look and you look and nowhere can you find,
What is needed to calm your spirit and the mind?
Then you remember something that sounded so right.
Study the word it's your guiding light.

Looking in God's Bible, you search, and you seek.
For something to give you strength since you feel so weak.
All of a sudden your eyes open and you finally see.
The good book's knowledge enlightens you with joy and glee,
That's how I can renew my strength and my might.
Study the word it's your guiding light.

The word is a light unto your path to direct and to lead.
Just open up the book and start to read.
The spirit will energize, and you will begin to rewind.
The instruction says seek, ask, knock and truth you will find.
Your understanding becomes so clear sunshiny and bright.
Study the word it's your guiding light.

The Holy Spirit begins to guide and to teach.
Higher heights with praise and lifted hands you can reach.
An enlightened mind with brilliance begins to exhilarate.
Knowledge and understanding come through your eye and ear gate.
You don't have to stay in a frightfully dark and fateful night.
Study the word it's your guiding light.

Poetry Reflections

1. **Inspirational Affirmations**

   _____
   _____
   _____
   _____
   _____

2. **Self -Reflections (consolation, comfort, conviction, connections, etc.)**_____

   _____
   _____
   _____
   _____
   _____

3. **Scripture Reflection**_____

   _____
   _____
   _____
   _____

4. **Implementation (goal setting)**
   Self_____

   _____
   _____
   _____
   _____

   Others_____

   _____
   _____
   _____
   _____

   Prayer of Thanksgiving & Praise_____

   _____
   _____
   _____
   _____
   _____

Praise and Worship

To appoint unto them that mourn in Zion, to
give unto beauty for ashes, the oil of joy for mourning,
the garment of praise for the spirit of heaviness, that they
might be called trees of righteousness, the planting of the Lord
that he might be glorified.

Isaiah 61:3 KJV

Praise and Worship Word Message

PROCLAIM POWERFUL PASSIONATE PRAISE
RAISE & LIFT HOLY HELPING HANDS
ADORE THE LORD PRAY & CONSECRATE
IGNIITE HOLY FIRE WITH A HALLUYAH SHOUT
SING SPIRITUAL HARMONIOUS SONGS
ENTER INTO HIS GATES WITH THANKSGIVING

Hallelujah Hallelujah Give God the Highest Praise

Lift up your voice to the God who is great.
The one above all from whom we radiate.
He is the creator of the heaven and of the earth.
For everything that exists he gave birth.
Night created and the days as a shining blaze.
Hallelujah, hallelujah, give God the highest praise!

Our mighty God separated water from dry land.
He creatively designed his great and grand plan.
Plants and fruits provided for mankind to eat.
All of this was a part of his awesome fantastic feat.
God saw it was good on each of the defined days.
Hallelujah, hallelujah, give God the highest praise!

He set up in the heavens the high reaching bars.
As he created the sun, moon, and twinkling stars,
He marked the cycles of months, seasons, and years.
As the heavens declared his Glory with radiating cheers.
The magnificent work of his hands with awe upon it we gaze.
Hallelujah, hallelujah, give God the highest praise!

Finally water creatures, birds and animals each of a different kind,
Came from God's dynamic and picturesque mind,
Man and woman he created with dominion and to obey.
Through deception and disobedience, they fell by the way.
A merciful loving God restores with the grace that amaze.
Hallelujah, hallelujah, give God the highest praise!

Come to God in Reverential Awesome

Unto him who is Lord of Lords and King of Kings.
Out of our hearts of melodies, we should begin to sing.
With soul, mind, and body before him, we must bow.
As our fearful respect heralds out wow oh wow.
In his light our unworthiness and sin we say confess, confess.
As we come to God in reverential awesomeness.

Our confession of repentant sins has made us divinely clean.
Now a portion of light begins to glow and in us shine and gleam.
God only do we begin to worship and gratefully praise.
With a shout of thanksgiving and hands lifted in a high craze,
We're saturated in his pure atmosphere and his pure holiness.
Therefore we come to God in reverential awesomeness.

We bring our temples, our altars, and make our sacrifice.
For Jesus on the cross paid the ultimate costly and valuable price.
We surrender our will and body as an offering of love.
Our best gifts we cheerfully bring to him who sits high above.
With devotions and dedication which we humbly express,
As we come to God in reverential awesomeness.

With a hallelujah shout, we adore and adore.
Wishing we could abundantly do even more and more,
His glorious cloud of splendor envelopes us all around.
And we fall in humility on his most holy ground.
We know that in his presence we have been spiritually blessed.
We came to a holy God in reverential awesomeness.

Come Before His Presence with a Melodious Song to Sing

Unto him, my heart has opened to receive.
For to him, I have come to believe,
I will enter into his gates with thanksgiving.
I owe only to him the blessed life I'm living.
As a testimony unto him myself I will bring.
Coming before his presence with a song I will sing.

I will enter into his gates with praise.
For the wondrous works, he displays.
Making a joyful noise with a loud sounding voice,
With a spiritual mouth poised to rejoice.
Because I've been delivered from sins deadly sting,
I come before his presence with a melodious song to sing.

As I bless Jesus, I will exalt his name.
He is highly proclaimed in the Bible's Hall of Fame.
Rejoicing in dance, and a praising shout, shout, shout,
Gladness fills the atmosphere with power and clout.
Instruments are magnifying with percussions and string,
Come before his presence with a melodious song to sing.

I will lift up high each holy and anointed hand.
For the Lord standing in heaven so tremendous and so grand,
He was crucified, resurrected, and for us, he was raised.
For this, he must be highly and wonderfully praised
He is our Lord, Savior, Deliverer, and King.
I come before his presence with a melodious song to sing.

Rejoicing in Him Is a Wonderful Delight

I praise God from whom my blessings flow.
Unto him I trust the best help I'll ever know.
My shield and my comforter I know no other.
Not bound by flesh you can't find another.
I see my blessings shining oh so bright.
Rejoicing in him is a wonderful delight.

My heart thirst for a full righteous soak
As I wrap myself in the dampness of a spiritual cloak,
Drenching in the overflow of an eye dripping tear,
My body does not feel overwhelming chills of fear.
I try to find him in the darkness of the night.
Rejoicing in him is a wonderful delight.

I sit low, but my eyes look to heaven so high.
If I had wings to him, I would swiftly fly,
This Lord who walked lowly on earth as a miracle maker,
He ranks above all as a mover and a shaker.
He denounced all wrong by revealing what was right.
Rejoicing in him is a wonderful delight.

I see in him the father, son, and the Holy Ghost.
He set the spiritual table as a gracious King and beloved host.
From him has come every good and perfect gift to each of us.
That's why he's the one we can always faithfully trust.
Oh, just to behold him will be a beautiful visionary sight.
Rejoicing in him is a wonderful delight.

Think on These Godly Things

When you see a fantastic tall Cedar Tree,
Think of God's unconditional Love for you and me.
You saw the leaves from the wind as it whistled and blew.
Think of his word which is everlastingly true.
When you hear the sounds of birds who daily sings,
Keep on thinking on these Godly things.

When you gaze at the tall snowcapped mountain peak,
Think of God's grace for the lonely, tired and weak.
When you see people marching and upholding for the just,
Think about Jesus whom you can faithfully trust.
When you see the eagle's strong flying wings,
Always remember to think on Godly things.

When you see a hornet full of buzzing bees,
Think of a good report of pure honey not hurting stings.
When you see a stream moving clear and free,
Think of a pure heart flowing in you and me.
When enlightened minds chime and goodness rings,
Daily begin to think on Godly things.

When you look at lovely flowers for your eyes to see,
Think about God's vision of what fragile beauty should be.
When you see the grass of a different green hue,
Think of how uniquely he created me and you.
Spiritually see jeweled crowns from the King of Kings.
This gift will be worth thinking on Godly things.

God's Glory Cloud

As I sit in my moment of still consecration.
I think of God and our spiritual relation.
Because my numerous sins have been lovingly lifted,
I know now that I have become spiritually gifted.
It's personal for me because I'm just not part of the crowd.
I have entered into God's Glory cloud.

As I move toward the illumination of his light,
The beauty is magnified and oh so bright.
The old has been washed away, and now I have a new story.
Because of the countenance of his eternal Glory,
As he moves quickly and quietly without sounds so loud.
I have entered into God's Glory cloud.

My heart radiates from his microscopic envelopment of perfection.
He's purifying me because I need his Holy correction.
It causes me to look up with great, awesome delight.
When I saw Holiness and everything appearing oh so right,
Being formed by him makes me joyous grateful and proud.
I have entered into God's Glory cloud.

In his presence, it's him indeed that I adore.
My love for him grows above measure more and more.
I behold him as I see the radiance glowing from his face.
My very being is filled with the honor of his exalted beaming grace.
I fall to my knee, and I humbly bow to the ground.
I have entered into God's Glory cloud.

Sacred Solitude

Oh, the stillness and quietness found present in God's holiness,
Our soul can feel a calmness of sweet blessedness,
When others are not physically present or around,
You can move into the presence of a soft musical sound.
You even fail to notice when others begin to intrude.
You have found the place of sacred solitude.

You begin to focus and try to clear your mind.
From the daily hustle and bustle, you begin to rewind.
Jesus in his glory you seek and fall on your knee.
The worries and troubles you're now spiritually set free.
From the toxic of people so unkind, crude and rude,
You've found the place of sacred solitude.

Your favorite scripture you inwardly quote.
The promises in the bible that God's prophets wrote,
Only good and happy thoughts you now begin to see.
Your heart starts to skip with joy, peace, and glee.
A cloud of spiritual softness also has changed your mood.
You found your place of sacred solitude.

This place of worship you want to remain.
With such bliss, you want refreshing like falling rain,
Feeling like a fluttering butterfly and a bird set free.
As the wind softly whispers through the leaves of a tree,
To be in his presence, you should more frequently isolate and seclude.
So you can find your place of sacred solitude.

Victory in Jesus the One We Trust

Jesus gave his life for you and me.
From the sting of death, we've been set free.
Eternal life is a gift for me and you.
Receiving it is all you have to do.
For all who believe with faith, it's a plus, plus, plus.
Victory in Jesus the one we trust.

Give praise now and don't delay.
As we remember those, who have gone their way.
They believed a long time ago and received their grace.
Now they can see Jesus face to face.
The end for the redeemed is not dust to dust.
Victory in Jesus the one we trust.

With hope in our hearts, we believe the son.
Victory for them has now been won.
No more sorrow and no more pain.
Now heaven has become their gain.
Life had many minus now it's a plus, plus, plus.
Victory in Jesus the one we trust.

One thing we know is that we all must die.
But there is something higher than pie in the sky.
There are jeweled treasures in the crown.
For those who are traveling and are heaven bound.
Regeneration and repentance have made Glory a must.
Victory in Jesus the one we trust.

Poetry Reflections

1. **Inspirational Affirmations**

   _____
   _____
   _____
   _____
   _____

2. **Self -Reflections (consolation, comfort, conviction, connections, etc.)_____**

   _____
   _____
   _____
   _____
   _____

3. **Scripture Reflection_____**

   _____
   _____
   _____
   _____
   _____

4. **Implementation (goal setting)**
   Self_____

   _____
   _____
   _____
   _____

   Others_____

   _____
   _____
   _____
   _____

   Prayer of Thanksgiving & Praise_____

   _____
   _____
   _____
   _____

Events And Tributes
"HATꟄ OFF"

Honor all men. Love the brotherhood. Fear God.
Honor the King.
1Peter 2 KJV

Events and Tributes Word Message

TIMES FOR CELEBRATIONS
REWARD THE RIGHTEOUS
IMPART HONOR TO WHOM HONOR ID DUE
BUILD UP AND ESTEEM OTHERS
UNITE& FELLOWSHIP WITH FAMILY & FRIENDS
TRADITIONALIZE SPECIAL OCASSIONS
EXHORT THE LORD IN ALL THAT YOU DO
SALUTE THE HUMBLED ACCOMPLISHED

Birthday Celebration

Another year of life in God's great land,
Continues your journey with his great plan.
A thousand years ahead starts with one step.
Rejuvenating you with an energizing pep.
Rejoicing another great day of lively sensation.
Hurray it's another birthday celebration.

So take time to delight in God and always pray.
It will make you strong enough to face each day.
Take each new day as your daily bread.
Now you can read God's word faithfully to be fed.
Observe the beauty of nature as you slowly tread.
A new birthday celebration that will make you glad.

It's time to laugh and have fun with friends.
Smiling with humorous jokes and facial grins.
Playing and winning game after game.
It's your birthday a time for fame.
We give God glorious adoration.
For a great birthday celebration.

Have faith when you turn and look ahead.
Order your step in the word and grow with God's bread.
New blessings will continue to come your way.
Be thankful and rejoice for each new dawning day
Move forward and upward toward God's high ground.
Let's praise and celebrate with a Hallelujah sound.

Happy Birthday Senior Let's Celebrate!

Celebrate today with a great cheer.
For you have been blessed with another year,
Going uphill can seem just a little rough,
But wisdom and knowledge gained will be more than enough.
Teach and train others and positively motivate.
Happy Birthday, senior let's celebrate!

You still have style and plenty of grace.
With a glow from within that, no one can erase.
So take your pill of consecration and don't cease to pray.
They'll make you keen to face and conquer each and every day.
Share the Love in your heart and daily meditate.
Happy Birthday, senior let's celebrate!

The new teeth you will wear are really your own.
Bought and paid for with cash or a loan.
You'll have your smile back so open real wide.
And show everybody the beauty inside.
No more yellow just the pearly white.
My oh my, what a glowing sight.

Don't with regret turn and look back.
Just carefully move on and make a new track.
Now move forward and upward to the higher ground.
And praise God with a great Hallelujah sound.
Stay focused and walk to God's golden gate.
Happy Birthday, senior let's celebrate!

Happy Happy Birthday My Love

bee happy

When I met you oh so many years ago,
We were just teenagers just starting to grow.
Through the years we've grown together,
In sunshine and stormy weather,
To each other our love is true.
Happy happy birthday my love from me to you.

Now I look as we grow old.
We're as hard to break as fired gold.
Sometimes our days were dark and light.
But through it, all our light shines bright.
God put us together, and prayer brought us through.
Happy happy birthday my love from me to you.

Through many times of the thick and the thin,
God has always helped us with a prayer to win.
We've had many, many birthdays to celebrate.
Some big and small but each one just as great,
The years like a bird just flew, flew, and flew.
Happy, happy birthday my love from me to you.

Even with the graying, you look great now as well as then,
You're my husband, my love, and even my best friend.
We will until death stand by each others side.
With our love growing as the ocean is wide.
You're not too old to me you're still fresh and new.
Happy, happy birthday my love from me to you.

A Special Birthday for You

In your mother's womb, you were made one of a kind.
Not another like you can anyone find.
Your mother pulled you to her so close and near.
She gave a shout and a marvelous loud cheer.
Every day has brought something unique and new.
But nothing is better than a special birthday just for you.

We watched you move from the baby's rattle.
Observing you moving into life's arena for battle,
You learned that life included a tough fight.
But you would gain a victory from God's might
You've fought a good fight while going through.
That's why we're celebrating a special birthday just for you.

God's rebirth has brought you from a child to an adult.
And what we see years later is a beautiful result.
You learned how to do good and treat people right.
By showing the radiance of righteous light,
We gave you the love of God so tender and true.
As we give a salute on this a special birthday just for you.

Each day you've lived part of God's purpose and plan.
Blessing others sometimes small and sometimes grand,
As you grow older and mature day by day.
You can guide others with the beams of a bright sunray.
Many more years we hope you are due.
As we say a special birthday, sincerely just for you.

Thinking of You the Oldest Birthday

During the times when you come to my mind,
A memory comes recalling a funny time.
A giggle, a smile, and a laugh comes through,
It's a delight to me when I think of you.

A sense of humor you always display.
Even on a cloudy, rainy or stormy day.
Some of the things you used to say and do,
It is enlightening to me when I think of you.

I think of those you stood by through thick and thin.
I know it wasn't easy, but you did it again and again.
Your husband you cared for with loving kindness so true.
It is inspiring to me when I think of you.

You've got a birthday that will soon be here.
Making you still the oldest, who we all hold dear.
Seeing you would be a bright day for the whole happy crew.
You're shining like starlights when I think of you.

We've got celebrations in Spring, Summer, Fall, and Winter.
Birthday and anniversary are days we always remember.
We'd love to see you and give honor to you because it's due.
And brighten our atmosphere as we celebrate what we think of you.

Love Acts Showing Valentine Care

When you look in this love sack,
You'll find your favorite tasty snack.
My handsome hunk, I chose them especially for you.
Because my Love for you is as strong as a coffee brew,
This is just for you only and not to share.
This is my love act showing valentine care.

I put in a forbidden no, no, treat.
A few pieces of chocolate bits dark and sweet,
For this is my greatest act which is my delight.
To help you feel loved with each delicious bite.
You and I both will eat as a sweet love pair.
This is my love act showing valentine care.

Today I need your twelve hugs, just for me.
Instead of twelve roses that are pretty to see.
I need your arms around me tight and warm.
Which for many years you've been my only charm.
My Love for you I verbally and romantically declare.
This is my love act showing valentine care.

So maybe on this exceptional night,
Without any fuss or without any verbal fight,
Let's find a good movie we can watch together,
On this valentine with sunshiny weather,
We will both sit with popcorn in our favorite chair.
This is my love act showing valentine care.

At the close of this beautiful love day,
We can end by cuddling in our own particular way.
And say thanks to our heavenly God above.
As we share with each other our enduring Love.
Knowing God has given us something very rare.
These are our love acts s showing our valentine care.

Resurrection Day

Celebration time is ever so near.
With Love in our hearts ever so dear,
Jesus Love was so great and divine,
His Love, Agape Love, was one of a kind.
A sacrificial price was required to pay
As we remember, Resurrection Day.

Jesus gave his life for you and me.
From the sting of death, we've been set free.
For all who believe with faith and trust,
Eternal life is for each of us.
Give praise now and don't delay.
As we remember, Resurrection Day.

The cross brought sorrow, suffering, and pain.
Bringing life everlasting is our gain,
On Calvary, he lovingly chose to die,
Delivered from sin, we can now fly high.
His light shines in darkness as the brightest ray.
As we remember, Resurrection Day.

Our sin and darkness were laid on the son.
Victory for us has been won.
With hope in our hearts, we run this race.
It's given to us through mercy and grace.
He went to the grave but didn't stay.
As we remember Resurrection Day.

This Season Let Us Give, Dance And Joyously Sing

The world has to take time to recognize this season and stop.
To think it's just not a time to shop, shop, shop.
But it's time to celebrate our Savior and, our King.
With gifts of love to others, we joyfully bring.
With hearts rejoicing like angels shout with bells to ring.
This season let us give, dance, and joyously sing!

Hope was given to the lost, the hurting and the forlorn.
On the starry night when Jesus Christ was born,
The world was brought out of the darkness and out of sin.
God has given us victory to overcome and to win.
A shining radiant and illuminating light he did bring.
This season let us give, dance and joyously sing!

To us, he has given peace, mercy, and grace that amazes.
For that, we give him worship, glory and high hallelujah praises.
A gift genuinely worthy of our belief and our trust,
Jesus is Savior, Messiah, Emmanuel, the God who is with us.
In adoration, we embrace his holy presence, and to him, we cling.
This season let us give, dance, and joyously sing!

Rejoice, rejoice let us all shout and celebrate!
Our Savior has come to us out of the heavenly gate.
He was born in Bethlehem on a silent and holy night.
Welcomed by the Angelic choir to earth as our glorious light,
He is Prince of Peace, Wonderful Counselor, Almighty God, and King.
This season let us give! Let us dance! Let us joyously sing!

We Say Thank You

The heart of God is visible each day.
Through his children in what we do and say,
You have shined so brightly with love still new.
We stopped to take time to say a loving Thank You.

You came to us during a time of great need.
The kindness you brought will blossom from your seed.
It's not just the things we say but what we do.
We say from our hearts of love a special Thank You.

It delighted our hearts during the night and the morn.
Like an expectancy of hope seeking to be born.
Our gladness, glee, and praise only God truly knew.
Again to each of you, we say Thank You.

It's good when you don't have to ask, but others just know.
And the Spirit says let's get up and make our lives show.
Love in action is as fresh as the morning dew.
We see God in you, and we say Thank You.

Continue to lift words of prayer up for us.
That in God with faith we will patiently trust.
Pray for strength and his guidance we will pursue.
As you lift us up, we say Thank You, Thank You.

So when trials and tribulations come your way.
We will with the same love to you repay.
With the light of the Lord to help you get through,
From our hearts of joy, we say Thank You, Thank You.

A Great Family Affair

It's always excellent and terrific to go down memory lane.
And get on with others who boarded this old family train.
Boarding with relatives like aunts, uncles, granny grans, and papas too,
Trailblazers clearing the path for relatives like me and you.
Now that great legacy we can now lovingly share.
For we now celebrate a grand family affair.

Some we did not recognize, remember or even know.
But we could feel the warmth and see God's Glorious glow.
Reaching out hands quickly to meet and to greet,
Getting to know each other face to face was a wonderful treat.
I no longer have to just look with just a curious stare,
For we now celebrate a grand family affair.

Some physical similarities seem to look a little like me.
I guess because we came from the same ancestral tree.
Even some of the talents seem to be the same,
Because we're descended from a great lineage name,
We are all here together; this shows that we genuinely care.
So now let's celebrate a grand family affair.

It's always good to know from whence we came.
We're proud to be a part of the DNA that runs through our vein.
Heads and hands are held high to God who gave us the root.
We are all branches and offsprings from the same heritage shoot.
Their light still shines through us with a gleaming Godly glare.
So now celebrate, celebrate a grand family affair!

This Time of Fellowship is the Cement of a Loving Relation

People gathered full of common times for fun and sharing.
Brings happiness and laughter with bonds of caring.
Celebrating, joking and playing games together.
In good and fiery times of gusty stormy weather,
The love of friends and family full of great appreciation,
This time of fellowship is the cement of a loving relation.

It's a time of kinship and flowing songs of praise.
Smiles of a radiant glow shining are on each face.
Solos and choirs singing from the old songs to the new,
Old school and new school enjoying the musical review,
With children and adults, representing many generations,
This time of fellowship is the cement of a loving relation.

Kinship with love bonding an acceptance to this unity crew,
Increases the fun loving crowd with more than just a few,
Traveling the hustle and bustle from far and near,
To be with other friends and family who are oh so dear,
Making the home of love their temporary destination,
This time of fellowship is the cement of a loving relation.

We remember the times of loss whose footsteps we now tread.
God in this group keeps the joy of laughter and soothes the sad.
Talking with the sick, and well and the young and the old,
They each share a story that needed to be told.
Just like the old country church with a full day congregation.
This time of fellowship is the cement of a loving relation.

Love Links Your Marriage for a Lifetime

A beautiful couple I know you will be.
Because of the glowing light in your eyes, we can see.
Moments of quality time that's designed and specially cut,
It will keep your marriage out of a deep dry rut.
You chose each other while you were still in your prime.
Love will link your marriage for a lifetime.

Moments of prayer time with a tick-tock when you're on a limb,
It will keep your marriage life from going dim.
Caring for each other with a God-given love,
Keeps your marriage vows with help from above.
Each year of the future with the trust you will climb.
Love will link your marriage for a lifetime.

Your feelings you should always quickly communicate.
When you disagree set the alarm and do not prolong the wait.
Use the Bible's knowledge, and understanding of being wise,
It will always help you clearly see a way to compromise.
God's Glass X will help clean dirty words and offensive grime.
Love will link your marriage for a lifetime.

The clock is beginning quickly to wind down.
Respect and affection you both have found.
Connect with God every second, minute, and hour.
And you will grow strong together with mighty power.
Wedding bells will soon begin to chime.
Love will link your marriage for a lifetime.

Congratulations, at Last, You Can Graduate

Farewell! Farewell! You have worked for so long.
You look now and wonder oh my where has the time gone.
Sometimes you worked hard and did your best,
And you studied enough to pass your hardest test.
Sometimes you were early, and sometimes you were late.
Congratulations, at last, you can graduate.

Look around and see who you need to thank,
Mom, dad, grandma, papa, and relatives who filled the gas tank,
The friend who tutored to help you make the grade,
And the coach who pushed you when you were unsure and afraid,
Don't forget the teacher who helped you determine your fate.
Congratulations, at last, you can graduate.

The custodian and guards who watched you in the hall,
And corrected you when they saw you about to fall,
The cafeteria workers when you were late and didn't get to eat,
Who gave you food and led you to a cafeteria seat,
They didn't even charge you for the food on your plate,
Congratulations, at last, you can graduate.

Thank the principal who could have sent you home.
For he knew that only in the streets would you walk and roam,
And for all of those who did not give up on you.
They saw the potential as you matured and grew,
God had your back knowing you could be the first rate.
Congratulations, at last, you can graduate.

Rest and Relax Your Retirement is Here

Work for you has served its place.
You were dedicated and committed to the jobs work race.
But there's a new chapter in your life now.
And you can shout joyfully wow oh wow.
Look hopefully forward and not to the rear.
Rest and relax your retirement is here.

You no longer have to wait for the alarm to ring.
Just lie there in bed and listen to the birds' sing.
Don't worry about the snow, storm, and rain,
Or even the slight headache when you headed to work in pain.
Concentrate on travel and visiting places far and near.
Rest and relax your retirement is here.

Work has developed your talents and gift.
Now you can reach out to others and lift.
Serving your community can bring happiness and joy.
As you help each man, woman, girl, and boy.
By being a part of wiping someone's sorrowful tear.
Rest and relax your retirement is here.

It's time to quiet your body, spirit, and mind.
Taking time to release stress and daily unwind.
Read God's word and on your blessings meditate.
Talk with God who rested as you devotionally relate.
Rejuvenate yourself with a hallelujah cheer.
Rest and relax your retirement is here.

A Strong Father

A strong father stands like a rock so very strong.
He stands for right even when his child is wrong.
A strong father stands high, and he stands tall.
Not in stature but as a firm disciplinarian wall.
With a voice carrying authority like the sound of a lions roar
Knowing one day, it will help you to soar.

A strong father takes his daughter out on her very first date.
So she can choose a boyfriend or a husband who is first-rate
A ball he places in the hands of his son.
Teaching that when he loses, in father's eyesight he's still # one.
A strong father says it's alright to cry when you are sad.
I'm here to help you laugh again and become gleeful and glad.

A strong father can admit that he has made a mistake.
But like fragile glass, you don't have to break.
He's right there to pick you up whenever you fall.
He'll hear and come running when he hears your call.
When decisions you make are unfruitful and weak,
Together with solutions, you can reach a new peak.

A strong father's unconditional Love from his heart he will show.
Knowing from up and down experiences you will surely grow.
Together with a strong dad and Father God hand in hand,
As you stumble through life's problems, he will help you to stand.
Maybe dad didn't know all of this to do.
But now you can return the good seeds he sowed in you.

Poetry Reflections

1. **Inspirational Affirmations**

    _____
    _____
    _____
    _____
    _____

2. **Self -Reflections (consolation, comfort, conviction, connections, etc.)**_____

    _____
    _____
    _____
    _____
    _____

3. **Scripture Reflection**_____

    _____
    _____
    _____
    _____
    _____

4. **Implementation (goal setting)**
    Self_____

    _____
    _____
    _____
    _____

    Others_____

    _____
    _____
    _____
    _____
    _____

    Prayer of Thanksgiving & Praise_____

    _____
    _____
    _____
    _____

"A **Star** is Born"

I praise you because I am fearfully and wonderfully made; your works are wonderful, I know that full well.
Psalm 139:14 NIV

Conclusion

The Bible is the key to filling your mind with the beauty that it was intended. This illuminating focus will help us to enjoy and see this spectacular manifestation. It will produce a fruitful, fulfilling life. Conflicts are inevitable because we live in a fallen world, but we have been given the tools that will help us to be overcomers. We will be victorious because we are with equipped powerful tools.

I desire that the poems in this book touch your spirit, mind, and body. Your attitude and fruit can be developed and shared with others. Your emotions and motivation will find its outlet and help you to move forward step by step and day by day. Fill your mind with knowledge and seek the wisdom that comes from God. You will gradually learn about the source of your faith and hope. When you understand that this is not highlighted in ignorance but in truth. This truth will set you free from physical, spiritual, and emotional bondage and you will be able to give God the highest praise(Hallelujah). Let's celebrate and give tribute to God!!!!

I desire that your BLESSINGS are BRIGHT when you feel BRUISED and BROKEN. Remember Believing is the BREAKING force to isolate and BEAT the problems and person of the issues that come into our lives.

The BIBLE is our encourager, and the poetry in this book is BIBLE BASED. May God bless you and the lives will be touched by you.

Bible Based Truths Highlighted in Poetry

BLESSINGS
IMPUTED
BRINGING
LOVE
EVERLASTING

BRUISED
INJURED
BLIND
LIVES
ESCAPING EARTH

BRIGHT
ILLUMINATING
BREATHTAKING
LIGHTS OF
ETERNITY

BROKEN AND
INFUSED WITH
BREAD OF
LIFE
ETERNALLY

BELEIVING
INSPIRATIONAL
BENEFITS
LIBERALLY
ESTABLISHD

BREAKING
INFECTIOUS
BONDAGE BY
LIBERATING AND
ERADICATING

BEELZEBUB ISOLATED BEATEN LIFELESS ENDING EVIL

Poetry Reflections

1. **Inspirational Affirmations**

   _____
   _____
   _____
   _____
   _____

2. **Self -Reflections (consolation, comfort, conviction, connections, etc.)**_____

   _____
   _____
   _____
   _____
   _____

3. **Scripture Reflection**_____

   _____
   _____
   _____
   _____
   _____

4. **Implementation (goal setting)**
   Self_____

   _____
   _____
   _____
   _____

   Others_____

   _____
   _____
   _____
   _____

   Prayer of Thanksgiving & Praise_____

   _____
   _____
   _____
   _____

Support Groups Poetic Beneficial Resource

1. **Speaking Engagements**
   Hospital Staff
   School Counselors & Teachers
   Church Pastors Teachers & Counselors
   Mental Health Professionals

2. **Places**
   Schools
   Hospitals
   Churches
   Mental Health Institutions
   Prisons
   Nursing Homes

3. **Individual & Small Support Groups for Children**
   ADHD
   Autism
   Bipolar Disorder
   Conduct Disorder
   Depression
   Grief
   Suicide
   Substance Abuse

4. **Individual & Small Support Groups for Adults**
   Anxiety Disorders Suicide Prevention
   Schizophrenia
   Attention Deficit/Hyperactivity
   Eating Disorders
   Depression
   Autism Spectrum Disorder
   Post - Traumatic Stress Disorder
   Bipolar Disorder
   Obsessive-Compulsive Disorder
   Borderline Personality Disorder
   ETC.

About the Author

Warren Jean Rouse has worked with children, youth and their families for over fifty years in academics, social skills, personal needs, and emotional trauma as an educator, school counselor, and volunteer. She has worked in the schools, church and community organizations. Mrs. Rouse is experienced in providing workshops and training locally and out of state for educators, counselors, and parents. She has served on community boards that are designed to help others and has written programs and grants in support of at-risk kids.

She was named Elementary Counselor of the Year for the Central Region and was nominated for the state and won the Arkansas School Counselor Association Elementary Counselor of the Year title for Arkansas.

After Mrs. Rouse retired, she went back to school to further her Christian education at GMOR Seminary Institute and received her doctorate in Christian Counseling just as she had received her Master's Degree in counseling for secular education. She is presently working on her Ph.D. in Christian Education, an unfinished degree before the doctorate in Christian Education.

Mrs. Rouse believes that her greatest degree is her BA Degree (Born Again) and without it, none of this would have been possible. She sometimes perceives her poetry as a continued opportunity to counsel and (Reach and Touch) in the written form of poetic expression.

Finally, at seventy-four years of age and nine years after retirement, she has published her first book. She desires that the anointing and prayers that she has prayed over this book will be a blessing, encouragement and a lift to the hearts of those who are hurting and burdened by the storms of life and the troubles of the world. As they meditate over the Godly words that have inspired her, prayerfully and hopefully they will also share the light of hope with others who are in stressful situations. Mrs. Rouse has been married for over 55 years to James D. Rouse Sr. and to this unit was born six children, ten grandchildren, and four great-grandchildren. Her motto is "To God Be the Glory for the Things He Has Done"! She presently lives in Little Rock, Arkansas.